How to Write an Essay in 5 Easy Steps

By Scribendi.com

Print Edition

ISBN: 1492338540
ISBN-13: 978-1492338543

CONTENTS

SCRIBENDI

INTRODUCTION

It's late at night; you're staring at your blank computer screen, and your essay is due *soon* . . .

It's worth a big chunk of your grade, but you're not sure exactly what your instructor wants . . .

You've done some reading and have some ideas about what to say, but you have *no* idea how to get it all organized . . .

If only you had started getting serious about this sooner . . .

Does any of this sound familiar?

It's okay; it's not your fault. Believe it or not, most people experience writing dread and find writing hard to do—including the pros who write for a living! Everyone procrastinates too, even when we know it's not the best approach to take.

It's probably also the case that no one has ever *really taught* you how to write an essay; it's just one of those skills you're supposed to have picked up along the way, right?

Do not fear: this guide will not only get you through the essay you have due *right now*, but will also provide a system that you can refer to again and again in the future. Here's what you'll learn:

1

1. How to figure out what your instructor wants from you

2. How to research your topic

3. How to organize all of those notes, thoughts, and ideas

4. How to actually write the essay

5. How to quickly edit your essay

Ready to begin? Let's go!

STEP ONE: FIGURING OUT WHAT YOUR INSTRUCTOR WANTS FROM YOU

When it comes to essay topics, there are only two possibilities: either you've been assigned a topic or you have to think of one yourself. This guide will provide tips for both of these options, and will then clearly explain how you can write a concise and powerful thesis statement that gives your instructor what he or she is looking for.

You have been assigned a topic . . .

In this case, your instructor has assigned a topic (or even a choice of topics), which means that you are limited in what you can write about. This can be a good thing, because you will know exactly what you should be researching, and essays with assigned topics are usually about the course material you're already familiar with. So even if the assignment doesn't thrill you, you've got a head start on the essay writing process.

. . . or you have to come up with your own topic

This one is a bit tougher. How do you narrow down the endless possibilities? Or, you might be wondering, how do you even figure out what the possibilities are?

Here are three places you can look to for immediate inspiration:

1. The course syllabus, catalog, or description. Sometimes, as we get bogged down in lectures and assigned readings, we forget what the *point* of the course we're taking is (especially if the instructor isn't great at lectures)! Almost every course has an overall theme or perspective that ties it all together. Take a quick look at the course web page or the catalog for reminders and some ideas of major themes.

2. General purpose reference books and sites. Encyclopedias and fact books provide thorough summaries and suggestions as well as related terms for sub-topics. Although you should never use these kinds of materials as sources in your final bibliography or reference list, they're great places to start. Try the following general resources, as they are quite global in scope:

> *i. The Oxford Companion to Politics of the World, which can be found in most college and university libraries*
>
> ii. CQ Researcher
>
> iii. Political Handbook of the World
>
> iv. The *Index to International Public Opinion, which can be found in most college and university libraries*
>
> v. World Opinion Update, which can be found in most college and university libraries

3. Google Scholar. Sure, everyone knows about Google's regular search tool, but do you know that there is a special sub-site solely for published academic papers? Google Scholar (http://scholar.google.com/) is a fantastic place to look for ideas because it finds the articles and letters that professors write for academic journals. In many cases, you'll only be able to see the abstract (also known as the summary) of the paper online, although your college or university library may have a copy of the full paper available, but the abstract is often enough to get your creative juices flowing.

i. Special note: Do not, under any circumstances, give in to the temptation to copy what you find. Remember, if you can find it online, so can your instructor. More to the point, plagiarism (copying and pasting material from sources and then pretending it's your own work) is wrong and can lead to serious consequences.

The secret to making your instructor happy

Do you know what every instructor in the world wants from you? He or she really, really wants you to do two things: Demonstrate that you have understood the course material and write intelligently about your subject

It's that simple! Use these points as guiding principles to narrow down the focus of your essay.

Bonus Tip: Be sure to pay particular attention to the keywords your professor uses in the assignment. Does he or she say "describe," "discuss," "evaluate," "compare," or "justify"? Make sure that you watch for these little words, as they will change the focus of your paper, and then you'll be all set to. . .

Create a powerful thesis statement

Before we explain how to write a thesis statement, it's important to note that there are a few different types of essays. Yes, as if writing an essay wasn't frustrating enough, now you have to make sure you are writing the *right type* of essay! There are **four** popular types of essays, and usually your professor will make it clear what type you should be writing.

1. The persuasive essay

As you may have guessed, the persuasive essay is one in which you are trying to persuade your reader (i.e., your prof) to adopt your stance on a particular issue. That's right; you are trying to prove that your argument is more valid than another argument. That doesn't mean you can just babble on and on about whatever you want, though. A persuasive essay's main argument must still be based on sound logic and you must use factual evidence (citations and references!) to support your claims.

2. The expository essay

Though it sounds more intimidating than the persuasive essay, the expository essay is really very straightforward. Essentially, you're writing a factual paper about your topic, without any (**any!**) of your own opinions. In fact, the use of first-person pronouns is not recommended. Keep this paper concise—meaning you need to get to the point and stick with it. Find evidence that supports your thesis (more references!) and present it clearly. Every sentence should have a purpose, and you are just providing evidence that supports your thesis statement. No fluff, no muss!

3. The narrative essay

The narrative essay is likely the most enjoyable of all essays that you have to write; the problem is that you probably won't *ever* be asked to write one in your university or college career. It is an uncommon essay selection. Nonetheless, it's still important to understand its requirements in the rare event you're assigned this type of essay. The narrative essay requires that you tell a story from a subjective point of view (you can even use "I").

4. The argumentative essay

This type of essay is very, very similar to the persuasive essay. The only distinct difference is that in an argumentative essay, you must make arguments for *and* against your viewpoint, meaning you are presenting both sides of the argument. The main intent of this type of essay is still to persuade the reader (your professor) to accept your argument; so, you must remember to explain why the views and evidence you provide in opposition to your argument are wrong (or have problems), and provide evidence that supports your main argument.

Now that you understand the four main types of essays, you need to focus on *exactly* how to write your thesis statement.

Keep in mind that thesis statements will change a bit depending on the type of essay you are writing, but the basic principles and structure stay the same. For the purposes of most university essays, all you need to know is that there are two parts to every A+ thesis statement; without these two parts, your professor may be confused as to what your argument is, and your grade will definitely suffer.

1. The first part of the thesis needs to be approximately 15 words or less and should explain exactly what the paper will discuss—the point of your essay.

2. The second part needs to outline exactly the basis of your argument. It is safe to assume that in most essays you will write early in your university or college career, you should use three arguments to support your major claim.

Your thesis statement must be specific, to the point, and concise. Do not use three words where one will do, and make sure anyone reading this statement will know exactly what the rest of your paper will say.

As a third-year university student, this writer wrote an essay about the shift in the agricultural landscape in North America since the 1920s. The essay received a grade of 92%, which was the highest mark in the class. Let's look at the thesis statement in this A+ paper:

> This essay will outline how traditional agriculture practices have shifted to form a new agricultural landscape, which promotes the monoculture of crops through the overuse of chemicals and the mechanization of labor, as well as how the fair trade movement has provided an opposing and alternative method of contemporary farming.

This thesis statement starts by explaining what the paper is about: the shift in North America's agricultural landscape is problematic.

It then outlines the writer's first two arguments: our current monoculture of crops exists because of the overuse of chemicals and the mechanization of labor.

Finally, it points out an alternative approach to solving this problem (the third argument): the fair trade movement provides an alternative method of contemporary farming.

Even after looking at this example, are you still worried that your thesis statement might be a dud? It will be if you do the following:

1. Your thesis will be a dud if you don't include your main argument and supporting points. In your thesis statement, you MUST explain what your paper is about and give a preview of your arguments.

2. Your thesis will be a dud if you forget to include it in the introduction of your essay. You MUST put your thesis statement in the introductory section of your essay. NEVER start the body of your essay without having explained your thesis.

3. Your thesis will be a dud if it is hard to understand because it is either too wordy or grammatically incorrect. You MUST make sure your thesis statement is clear and straight to the point. If it isn't understandable, the rest of your paper will be hard to follow. Think of your thesis statement as a movie trailer. If the movie trailer is bad or misleading, are you likely to go see the film and enjoy it? Probably not.

STEP TWO: RESEARCHING YOUR ESSAY

The top five places to find good resources fast

Okay, you've chosen your topic, and you've written your thesis statement, or at least, you have thought about what you want your paper to be about. Now it's time to find some valuable sources that will provide facts and evidence to support your arguments and allow you to slide into that top 10% of the class.

Let's look at five sources that you probably haven't thought about consulting when conducting your research.

1. Course materials

If you're writing an essay for an academic institution, chances are you have a course syllabus and have purchased the necessary reading materials for the course. This is a *gold mine*. Almost all essay assignments are based on the course material in one way or another, so one of your best resources will be your assigned course pack or reading list. Don't just settle for using course materials as your sources; look at the bibliographies and reference sections of these resources to see what journal articles and academic publications have been sourced by their writers. Investigate these sources and use them throughout your essay. Chances are your instructor thinks these are great resources; otherwise, he or she wouldn't have assigned them as reading materials!

2. Professor support

Most instructors will tell you that the students who typically do the best on essays are the ones who ask for help. It can be as simple as sending an email to your professor or teaching assistant (TA) and asking if you're on the right track. You can stop by during office hours with some of your ideas and ask if your professor or TA has any other thoughts or leads. Professors, and especially TAs, are there to help you, and they don't mind assisting you with your essay, as long as you bring it to them before the due date. This is the only resource that you cannot use the night before your paper is due, as it will alert your instructors and TAs to the fact that you procrastinated, and they may be less likely to offer a helping hand.

3. Your professor's work

Your professor is teaching the course you are enrolled in because he or she is considered to be an expert in that field—one of the best and brightest in that specific area of research. Don't be afraid to look through your professor's research to see how it fits into your essay. Also, look at other work from your department's faculty to see what their contributions to your area of study are. Indeed, your professor will take you sourcing his or her work as a compliment! One word of caution when sourcing your prof's work—make sure you fully understand the concepts being discussed, as no one knows the material better than your prof.

4. Wikipedia

Let's be very clear here: do not cite Wikipedia as a source of information. This is universally frowned upon. However, Wikipedia (and Google Scholar) can be a great starting point for your research. Type your essay's keywords into these sources and see what results come up. Wikipedia, in its references section, will typically provide you with the titles of numerous academic publications and/or journals on your topic, which you can then find. Both sites will also give you summaries and clear explanations of major theories/concepts and the work of scholars. Remember, do not cite these sources. They should be used as starting points for quickly finding very valuable resources.

5. Online university library resources

If you are writing this paper close to the deadline, then you likely don't have time to run over to the library and scan through multiple books and articles. However, that doesn't mean you can't find valuable resources from the online catalogs that your university or college has to offer. Go to your library's electronic databases, input your keywords, and—BAM!—within minutes, you will have hundreds of sources at your disposal. This may require a bit of sifting through, which is similar to physically doing the research at the library, but these are all electronic resources that can be accessed from the comfort of your own dorm room, the night before your paper is due.

How do I keep track of my sources?

An amazing thing has changed higher education: Students can now electronically record all of their sources in one program, and this software, which will be explained below, does all of the organizing for you. **Utilize this!** This is something far too many students don't use, and it's a real shame. Creating your bibliography will be one of the most time-consuming (and boring . . . and frustrating!) parts of writing university papers. And, let's face it, if your paper is due in the morning, you don't have an hour or two to worry about formatting and recording all of your sources manually, do you?

Aside from saving you time later, another major reason you should spend a bit more time entering your sources into these programs while doing your research is that it will keep you organized and make your essay writing process more efficient. Spend an hour or two (or more if you have the time!) doing your research in one sitting; enter all of your information into one of the programs described below, and then get to work. There is no sitting around trying to retrace your steps or remember where you put that pad of paper. This will save you a lot of time and keep you on track, helping you avoid becoming distracted and feeling overwhelmed.

Here are four good tools for rapid bookmarking and building a bibliography on the fly.

1. **Connotea** is a completely free online reference management system for students that requires no downloading. You just find a reference, enter its details into the program, and come back to it later. You can even organize this program by essay topics to ensure you aren't confusing citations from the many different papers you are bound to be writing during essay season!

2. **CiteULike** is a free service for managing and discovering scholarly references that allows you to store your references, search for new references, and trade references with peers who are studying in similar fields.

3. **Zotero** is also a free program that will help you collect, organize, cite, and share your references. It allows users to create a library of references that can be managed and, most importantly, specifically formatted.

4. **Mendeley Desktop**, unlike the previous programs, which are web based and fairly simple, is an independent program, featuring its own desktop icon. It can manage and store references, create bibliographies, and format references into specific styles. This isn't something that you should consider getting hours before your paper is due, as there just won't be time to learn how to use it. Consider getting this program prior to your essay's due date and learn how to use it; this will definitely save you time and energy when writing future papers.

Quick time-saving tip: If you have time to hit the library a day or two before your essay is due, don't just grab one or two books while you're there. Spend an hour doing quite a bit of research and then pick up several books all at once. The less frequently you have to visit the library, the better. It would be terrible if you went to the library and forgot to get a critical resource and didn't realize it until a few hours before your paper was due, at which time the library would be closed. Planning a bit better now will save you stress later!

Key factors in evaluating your new source

Once you've exhausted all research avenues, have a heap of stuff to review, and have entered your reference information into a citation software program to save you time later, start reviewing your resources. Depending on how much time you spent collecting good resources, this can be a painless or very, *very* painful process. If you spent a few hours and used the above suggestions, this should just be a matter of skimming through the work to get an understanding of the concepts/theories. If you haven't done good quality research already, you may have to backtrack in order to find better resources. Either way, don't give up! Here are some tips to make this process as easy as possible.

1. Skim through the resources

When working with a tight deadline, there is absolutely no time (or need) to read every word on every page of every resource you have. Doing so can take days, and quite frankly, probably will do more harm than good, as you will overanalyze the work and get bogged down by the small details that you may not understand. Skim through the resources to see the general ideas and how they fit into your arguments. After a few pages, you will have a good idea as to whether the resource is a keeper or should get tossed in the "See ya later" pile!

2. Look at the table of contents

Don't be afraid to read the table of contents thoroughly. Many students have found that a lot can be said in those short pages. Tables of contents are meant to help direct you to the sections of books that are most relevant to your work. Why read Chapter 2, which is about chicken farming, just because it comes before Chapter 5, which is the chapter that discusses crop farming in America—the material that is exactly what you need for your essay. Use the table of contents as a guide; it will save you time and headaches when reviewing your sources.

3. Does the resource support or refute your thesis?

Sometimes we get bogged down by a resource we really like, or a quote that sounds great, but it doesn't actually help further our argument or thesis. Delete it. Toss it. Get rid of it. When time is precious, don't get attached to resources or ideas that are not actually going to help your essay. When skimming through the resources, ask yourself this simple question: "Does this source help prove my point, or does it refute it?" If it helps prove your point, keep the resource and mark it accordingly. If it refutes your point, still keep the resource and mark it (as discussed earlier, in many essays you have to provide both sides of the argument). If it does neither, or if you don't think the arguments in it are as strong or convincing as those in other resources, don't spend precious minutes or hours trying to make the ideas work; put the resource in the reject pile and call it a day.

4. Annotate as you go

Although this might seem straightforward, countless students (even your instructor may have made this mistake once or twice) forget to make notes, and then spend hours trying to find the quote or section of a paper that they need. Save yourself the stress of doing this and make clear, short notes (accompanied by page numbers) on material from sections of books that you think you may need later. Spending a bit of time here will save you much more time later.

5. Quick time saving tip

This will be discussed a bit more in the next section, but you might consider color-coding arguments and notes. For example, if there are three main points in an essay, you could highlight one blue, one green, and one yellow. All the sources that help prove point one are highlighted in blue; point two, green; and so on. This technique saves a great deal of time down the road and is a really simple way to see what resources are adequate, what you may need to grab next, or what sections of the paper need a bit more research.

STEP THREE: ORGANIZING YOUR ESSAY

Don't skip this step!

You have chosen your topic, written a thesis statement (or thought about one), and completed the research and organized material according to related themes (color-coded, even). Now, it is time to sit down and actually organize and plan your essay. So many students skip this stage because they think it is pointless or a waste of time. *It is not!* This is a key step in writing a paper that is coherent and logically laid out—a paper that your professor or TA will read and be able to follow.

There is nothing worse than marking a student's paper and having to spend time trying to figure out what the point of the paper is, where the arguments start and finish, and what references prove which point. And yet, time after time, that is exactly what professors have to do. If you want your essay to stand out and for your professor to breathe a sigh of relief when reading your essay, do not skip building a quick outline. It makes all the difference. Your paper will be clearer, better organized, and more coherent. You will earn a better grade by taking an extra 15 or 20 minutes to organize your paper effectively.

How to quickly build an outline

Building an outline does not need to take hours. If you're writing your dissertation, yes, an outline will be an extremely detailed and comprehensive exercise. For the purposes of students writing essays, however, it can be as simple as outlining the introduction, main body, and conclusion.

The introduction

The introduction should be a relatively short paragraph or two introducing the topic in broad terms. If your paper is 3,000 words (or roughly 8–10 pages) long, approximately one to two pages should be dedicated to the introduction, as you are only outlining the topic in a general way. As discussed earlier, you must include your thesis statement at the end of your introduction, before your first detailed argument begins.

The main body

The main body of a 3,000 word essay should be approximately six to eight pages. It should be the longest section of your essay and it should reflect the greatest amount of research. Every paragraph should be focused on supporting your thesis. Even when you are providing evidence against your point, you should discuss how that point is valid, and then, for the purposes of your paper, refute it by showing that it is flawed in some way. Pointing out opposing arguments and discussing the faults in those arguments only makes your paper stronger. Leaving out evidence that contradicts your work is a mistake.

The body of your essay should also be broken down into paragraphs containing various arguments. If you are writing a traditional three-argument/three-point essay, you should have those clearly separated so that the reader can easily follow when you move from point one to point two and so on. You do not necessarily need only three paragraphs for three arguments, however. Sometimes, to be fully developed, argument one might require four paragraphs, while argument three might require only two. There is nothing wrong with that, as long as it is clear where your arguments shift.

On this note, it is important that you make your essay unified and coherent throughout all points of the essays. Don't dramatically change the language you are using or the sentence structure from one point to another. Using transitions ("firstly," "secondly," "moreover," "in addition to," etc.) is OK, but don't make them too formulaic or simplistic, and don't start every new point with a transitional phrase. At the university or college level, transitions should support content and be more sophisticated.

Conclusion

Similar to the introduction, the conclusion should be about a page long for a 3,000 word paper. The conclusion of your paper should not only briefly summarize what your paper was about, but should invite critical thinking or offer some sort of final thought. This can be done in a few short sentences in a shorter paper, but in a longer, more advanced essay, you may need to write pages. In the previously mentioned paper about the changing agricultural landscape in North America, the conclusion should offer some way to help change the existing situation or perhaps cite research that shows how reverting to more independent farming would be more lucrative.

Therefore, if you apply what you have learned about what each section of an essay should do, your outline will evolve from a more basic structure to one that is a little bit more detailed.

1. Introduction

a. Brief overview of the topic being discussed

b. Thesis statement

2. Main body

a. Point one supporting thesis

b. Point two supporting thesis

c. Point three supporting thesis

d. Points against thesis

3. Conclusion

a. Summary of arguments

b. Reiteration of thesis proved or disproved and thoughts for the future (concluding with a point that leaves the reader with something to think about or wanting to take some kind of action will impress your instructor)

When drafting your outline, quickly write down where your arguments go. This is where the color coding mentioned earlier can play an important role. If you color coded by argument when doing your research, it will be very easy, in the outlining stage, to insert your arguments (and refer to research that supports those arguments). Basically, creating an outline is like putting a puzzle together. You're taking all of the pieces we've discussed so far and putting them together in a logical way, so that they all fit. Do you see why this step is so important? If you don't take a few minutes to organize your paper and lay out your arguments, you'll either spend a lot of time later trying to find the missing pieces, or you'll have a final product that doesn't actually come together properly.

Example essay outline

1. Introduction

a. Brief description of topic being discussed

i. Agriculture in North America has changed dramatically since the 1920s, and for the past 40 years, the agriculture business has been dominated by large farms that typically specialize in growing a single cash crop.

ii. Internationally, the fair trade movement has significantly affected attempts to create an alternative to the current agricultural system.

iii. Sources (BLUE): Knight; NFFC; DeCarlo

b. Thesis statement

i. This essay will outline how traditional agricultural practices have shifted to form a new agricultural landscape, which promotes the monoculture of crops through the overuse of chemicals and the mechanization of labor, as well as how the fair trade movement has provided an opposing and alternative method to contemporary farming.

2. Main body

a. Point one supporting thesis

i. The new agricultural landscape will be outlined, specifically discussing the significance of monoculture crops and how chemicals assist in their production.

ii. Sources (GREEN): Pollan; Knight

b. Point two supporting thesis

i. The new agricultural landscape will be outlined, specifically discussing the significance of monoculture crops and how machines assist in their production.

ii. Sources: (BLUE) Berry; Knight

c. Point three supporting thesis

i. What farms will look like in the future if this continues and how the fair trade movement can prevent the monoculture of crops

ii. Sources (YELLOW): Koons; Berry; Knight; TransFair; Brown; Nicholls and Opal

3. Conclusion

a. Summary of arguments

i. The agricultural landscape has undergone a tremendous shift since World War II. This shift is continuing more and more each year with greater emphasis on monoculture cash crops, an increase in chemical and fertilizer use, and the mechanization of labor.

b. Reiteration of thesis proved or disproved and thoughts for the future

i. It is not known what is going to happen to the agricultural landscape; however, by purchasing fair trade certified products, consumers can ensure their voices are heard and they can make a difference in contemporary farming.

STEP FOUR: WRITING THE ESSAY

Putting flesh on the skeleton

Do you think it's impossible to have fun while writing an essay? Think again! Well . . . fine, it isn't everyone's cup of tea, so let's make this as painless as possible. Once you have your outline, it's time to put some meat on those bones. How do you come up with 8–10 pages from the one page outline? Here are four tips to help you:

1. Use quotations

It is totally unacceptable (and annoying for the person grading your paper) to fill your entire paper with direct quotations from your sources. However, that doesn't mean you have to come up with the greatest idea that ever hit the academic world either. Use the resources you found to provide evidence for your arguments. Use 1–3 short, direct quotations (with citations) on every page and then paraphrase (and cite what you paraphrase) several more times. Before you know it, much of your page is filled with content from sources, and it's your job to complete the discussion.

2. Use connecting sentences

There is nothing wrong with using a lot of sources, as long as they are logical, well thought out, and cited properly. In fact, this is encouraged in undergraduate degrees. Therefore, connect the thoughts of the academics you quote or paraphrase with sentences that flow well. It is even acceptable to summarize some of these key thoughts in the following sentence while directing the reader to the next point.

3. Make use of your notes

While skimming through your resources, you will have made notes. Remember to look back on those notes and make sure you are hitting all the key points. Sometimes, if you don't look back at your original notes, it is easy to miss an important argument or thought. These notes will also give you ideas for expanding your arguments when you seem to be drawing a blank. Refer to these notes often, as they are a valuable tool.

4. Follow your outline

No matter what happens, follow your outline. Don't go off on random tangents; stay on track, and keep your essay organized in a logical way. While writing your essay, you may realize that you want to add a key point, and that's totally fine! Just make sure you account for it in your outline and adjust the rest of your arguments appropriately to ensure that there isn't any repetition and that things still flow properly. You took the time to write this outline; you need to use it.

Remember to think about writing your essay as if you are filling in the blanks or adding a bit of meat to the bones. The hard work is already done: you have a topic and thesis statement, you've researched your paper and have good sources, and you've written a pretty good outline. Once all of this is done, putting pen to paper is easy!

Seven tips for clear writing

1. Log out of Facebook

You will be able to write so much more and so much better if you limit your distractions. Facebook is fun, but remember that you have a big essay due in a couple of hours. The penalty deducted from your grade each day that you are late is not worth staying logged into Facebook (or other sites like it) for a couple of hours.

2. Take a break every 45 minutes

Get up and stretch every 45 minutes or every hour just to get away from your essay and let your mind focus on something else. But don't let these breaks last too long; they should last just enough time to allow you to stop thinking about your paper and relax. Then, it's back to work!

3. Stay hydrated

You may not be physically running a marathon, but writing a 3,000 word essay in a few short hours is a mental marathon and requires you to stay alert. Make sure you're drinking some water or juice to stay hydrated and remain awake as the clock ticks away.

4. Stay on task

It can be very tempting to move onto the next point or section of the essay when you aren't finished with the first, but try to avoid doing so, if possible. You will feel much calmer and more relaxed if you finish a section, rather than frantically moving from one section to another. Stay focused and remember that you have the research done and can finish the current section before moving onto the next.

5. One paragraph, one point

Remember that every paragraph should only have one key point. This might sound obvious, but all too often, students forget that paragraphs are meant to represent one key thought supported by major and minor details. A new thought, point, or argument typically means a new paragraph.

6. Avoid tense shifts

Most professors and TAs agree that a major problem with undergraduate papers is that students tend to shift between tenses when it isn't necessary to do so. In addition, stick to the rule that personal pronouns should *always* be avoided.

7. Don't be too hard on yourself

Writing clearly and concisely isn't easy, and it is a skill that isn't typically developed until the third or fourth year of university. That being said, work hard at trying to make sure your points are clear and that you have only one idea in every paragraph; but also, give yourself a break. You aren't a master at writing yet, and no one expects you to be. Do your best, stay organized and focused, and you'll write a good quality paper.

Copy and paste = bad!

There tends to be some confusion at times about what plagiarism is. To be very clear:

- You cannot copy anyone's work, directly or indirectly, without giving credit to that person.

- You cannot take a direct quotation without saying where it is from and who wrote it.

- You cannot paraphrase what someone wrote without saying where it is from and who wrote it.

- You cannot copy and paste a blurb from the Internet without citing the source.

- You cannot take Wikipedia's definition of a word without saying where you got it (and remember, don't ever use a definition from Wikipedia!).

Plagiarism occurs when a writer, for whatever reason, consciously or unconsciously steals the work of another writer and passes it off as his or her own. The stolen material does not have to be taken verbatim, however; simply taking another writer's ideas and rephrasing them as one's own can be considered plagiarism as well if the source is not cited.

How citing works

Now that you know exactly what plagiarism is, it's important to outline exactly how you can cite properly to avoid plagiarism. If you're enrolled at an academic institution, you have likely heard of various style guides:

- *The Publication Manual of the American Psychological Association* (APA)

- *Modern Language Association* (MLA)

- *Chicago Manual of Style* (Chicago)

- *A Manual for Writers of Term Papers, Theses, and Dissertations (Turabian)*

Depending on the course, you will likely have to follow one of these style guides consistently throughout your paper. The links above will take you to articles that will help explain exactly how to cite using each of the style guides, and you are encouraged to read through these resources briefly before beginning to use your particular style guide. The most important thing to remember, however, is that you must properly attribute the works that you have consulted to their respective authors.

This is an example of a properly formatted citation in our example essay, which uses MLA style:

In addition to the reduction of manpower in the sector, the farming and meat processing jobs that are left in the agricultural sector are "two of the most dangerous and low-paying jobs in the United States" (Knight 190).

These are examples of the above source that are either **not** cited or are improperly cited:

In addition to the reduction of manpower in the sector, the farming and meat processing jobs that are left in the agricultural sector are "two of the most dangerous and low-paying jobs in the United States."

In addition to the reduction of manpower in the sector, the farming and meat processing jobs that are left in the agricultural sector are two of the most dangerous and low-paying jobs in the United States.

Do you see the difference? It really is that easy to make sure you avoid any allegations of plagiarism!

But no one will ever know

It is extremely stressful to be up hours before a big essay is due, still staring at a blank page. In addition, you have a lot riding on scoring a B on this essay—your scholarship, your parents' approval, admission into another program, or something else. Anyone who has been in that position understands that plagiarizing is tempting. Even some of your school personnel really do understand. However, as anyone who has had to confront students about plagiarism and see students lose their academic careers will tell you: plagiarizing is **never** worth it.

If you think it is easy to plagiarize, it is even easier for professors and TAs to catch students who do so. A change in the style of writing, a small font change, a slightly different font color on the page, an increase/decrease in spelling or grammatical errors, or a tone that is inconsistent with prior or later work are just some indicators of plagiarism. As well as you think you may be hiding the fact that you are plagiarizing, know that your professor has likely seen it all. Moreover, this doesn't even include the reality that many professors now make you turn your essay in to programs like TURNITIN, which scan your paper against databases to ensure originality.

If getting kicked out of university, never being able to apply to another university in the country, failing your course, and having your name tarnished are not enough reasons to prevent you from plagiarizing, maybe knowing that you stole someone's hard work is. In addition, knowing that you have worked hard on an essay, thesis, or report is extremely rewarding and may be sufficient reason. If you don't plagiarize, you will be able to explain every word of every essay you have ever written if asked. If questioned, you will be able to easily defend yourself against plagiarism. You don't want to be put on the spot and asked a question about your work that you are not able to answer. You don't want to go into an exam and not be able to answer the questions because there is no option to copy, and you haven't done the work yourself. Doing the work yourself and working hard at it will set you up to excel in more than just school; you will be better prepared for success in the work force as well.

STEP FIVE: REVISING YOUR ESSAY

There are a few things that can really prevent your essay from getting that A+. If it's three in the morning and you just finished writing your essay, head to bed for three hours, wake up at six, and quickly edit your essay before handing it in at 8:00 a.m. By doing so, you will catch mistakes, and your instructor will thank you for not submitting a paper riddled with spelling and grammar errors. If you can't see yourself waking up on time to edit your paper yourself, you can always turn to Scribendi.com and have the paper edited while you sleep.

The five most common things that kill essays

1. Passive voice

Do not use the passive voice when it can be avoided. The sentence "Tom punched Bob" is written in active voice; "Bob was punched by Tom" is in passive voice. Your high school English teacher was right: Passive voice does sound weak, and although it's okay sometimes, it should be used sparingly. And, often, using the passive voice leads to wordiness in your essay, which, as shown in the next point, you should also try to avoid. Active voice should always be your first choice!

2. Too many words/words you'd never use in real life

First, try to be concise and clear. If you can write a sentence in 10 words, but you're using 20, revise it! Your essay will sound stronger, and your instructor will appreciate your conciseness. Look for this when you're editing, and eliminate cases of wordiness. Second, sometimes our focus is so much on sounding as if we're intelligent that we lose track of what we're actually trying to say. Don't get caught up in using big words that most people never use. Use words that you understand and that fit in the sentences. You will appear more confident.

3. Redundancies

When you're writing quickly or forget to edit, you likely have some redundant information in your paper. You don't want to repeat the exact information time and time again. Yes, it's important to get your point across; but don't just summarize the same thing seven times to do so. For a more concise paper, avoid restating the same information.

4. Killer clichés and colloquialisms

Though these are very common in everyday language, they are frowned upon in academic writing (similar to personal pronouns). Do not use expressions like "If you know what I mean?" and entirely avoid using "like" (if you, *like*, enjoy coffee, you'll love this new brand at Tim Horton's) in your essays. If you say something like "This concept is really cool" in your essay, you will likely get called out for it by your instructor.

5. Vague wording

Don't use wording that doesn't have purpose or is unclear. Saying something like "Some people believe" is far less effective than saying "In the *Unsettling of America: Culture and Agriculture*, Wendell Berry argued that . . ." Being too vague will harm your essay, and this is something you should look out for when editing your essay.

If you revise your paper for these key points, you'll have a better essay, and your grade will reflect that. GrammarCamp.com provides comprehensive grammar training that will help improve your written communication skills. Turn to the example essay in the Appendix for more information. Appendix One offers a full-length example of an A+ paper, written in keeping with the five easy steps discussed earlier.

BONUS: HOW TO MAKE YOUR ESSAY STAND OUT

Pretend, for a moment, that you are the instructor, professor, or TA. You have 100 or 200 papers to grade, all on the same or similar topics. You have a week to read 600,000 words while still teaching and conducting your own research. You are not looking forward to reading these papers, especially when three quarters of them are poorly written. You're bored, exhausted, and frustrated by the quality of the papers you're getting.

How would you feel in the same position? What would make you happy? What would make you notice an essay and award the writer high marks?

You really need to stand back and ask yourself these questions, because that is what is going to make your instructor appreciate your work and remember it as being of high quality. Here are three tips that may help you secure higher grades.

Three easy ways to make your essay stand out

1. Follow the instructions

This may seem simple, but many readers of students' essays will tell you it is *rare* for students to follow the instructions. One way to ensure you avoid this tendency is to print out the guidelines your professor has given you, and after you finish editing your paper, quickly review them to be sure your work meets all the criteria.

a. If the word count is 3,000 words, submit roughly 3,000 words. Do not submit 2,500 and do not submit 3,500.

b. If the requirement is 10 academic sources, you must use 10 academic sources.

c. Be sure to follow your required style exactly. The title page, the page numbers, in-text citations, and references must follow the required style guide to the letter.

2. Use an acceptable font, and staple the pages of the essay

Again, these steps seem like common sense, but many students don't follow them. Font selection, color, and size are critical to keeping the person grading your paper happy. Your instructors/professors do not want to see size 14 fonts or grey fonts with a shadow behind the letters. Moreover, they certainly do not want to see a crazy, creative font. If you haven't been given instructions, and your style guide doesn't say, it is safe to stick with black font color, Times New Roman, and 12 point. Oh, one other quick tip: staple your papers together. Paper clips fall off and binders are bulky. Would you want to carry 200 pages of loose paper or bulky binders around campus? Probably not.

3. Practice the art of consistency

If you are going to use the term "website" (instead of "web site") in your paper, do it throughout the entire paper. If you are going to capitalize a word (whether it is right or wrong), do it throughout your paper. If you are using one particular style guide, use it throughout your paper. If you are listing three words in a sentence time and time again, put them in the same order (Bob likes bells, balls, and bats—bells should always be first, balls second, and bats third). If you are using Calibri font instead of Times New Roman, use it throughout the paper. There is nothing worse for instructors/professors than seeing inconsistency in the small details throughout students' papers. It gives the impression of a quickly put together essay and makes them question your research skills and attention to detail.

There you have it! We are actually done now. Now you are ready to go on and write that A+ paper by following these five easy steps.

APPENDIX ONE: EXAMPLE ESSAY

Example essay

The Fair Trade Movement Battles the Contemporary Agricultural
Landscape

Agriculture in North America has changed dramatically since the

1920s, and, for the past forty years, the agriculture business has been

dominated by large farms that typically specialize in growing a single

cash crop, whether it be "corn, rice, soybeans, tobacco, wheat, beef,

chicken, dairy, or pork" (Knight 184). The domination of the agricultural

landscape in North America by large farms reflects the fact that the

sector and the government no longer encourage or support small

privately owned family farms. The National Family Farm Coalition

(NFFC) argues that a family farm is

> not defined by size, but rather by the fact that the family
> provides the vast majority of the labor and management
> decisions . . . some [family farms] farm a couple of acres while
> others farm thousands of acres. The common goal of family
> farmers is farm sustainability—both economically and
> environmentally. (NFFC)

Although family farms make up about sixty percent of all farms in the

United States, the amount of cash crops produced—also known as the

output—by family farms is significantly less than that of their industrial

counterparts (Knight 191). Therefore, although family farms still exist in

the United States, they are not valued by the government or

supported—through tax cuts and subsidies—in the same way that the

larger farms are (NFFC). A family farmer is therefore "squeezed

between higher operating costs and what he gets for his produce; the

man on the farm must become more efficient or give up" (Berry 63). In

the agricultural business today, family farmers must "get big or get

out," making little room for family farms that grow a diversity of crops

(Knight 184). The change in the traditional agricultural landscape is

largely associated with increasing the efficiency of farming to create

larger quantities of cash crops. In *Supersizing Farms: The*

McDonaldization of Agriculture, Andrew Knight argued that, after World

War II, "for the first time ever, the focus was on agricultural productivity and globalization rather than on emphasizing meeting regional consumers' demands" (186).

Since agribusiness aims to make greater profits by becoming more and more efficient and by disregarding communities' and consumers' needs, the agricultural sector now works within a system that promotes the monoculture of crops through an increase in the use of chemicals and the mechanization of labor. Several social movements have been formed to fight the new agricultural landscape, including the National Family Farm Coalition, the organic movement, and the fair trade movement. Internationally, the most significant impact has been made by the fair trade movement in its attempts to create an alternative to the current agricultural system. *Fair trade* is defined as

> A trading partnership, based on dialogue, transparency, and respect, that seeks greater equity in international trade. It contributes to sustainable development by offering better trading conditions to and securing the rights of, marginalized producers and workers—especially in the South. Fair trade organizations are actively engaged in supporting producers, in awareness raising, and in campaigning for changes in the rules and practices of conventional international trade. (DeCarlo 3)

Fair trade, therefore, combats more than just trading practices. It focuses significant attention on the practices of production and actually advocates against the creation of a monoculture, the overuse of chemicals, and the mechanization of labor in agriculture. In *Fair Trade*, Jacqueline DeCarlo argues that, "in the new global economy, corporations from developed countries are increasingly moving their production to developing countries" (37). Accordingly, the new agribusiness that has changed the agricultural landscape in North America has also invaded many developing nations, which do not have the labor law enforcement or environmental restrictions that North America does. This situation creates an even worse system for agriculture in developing nations when compared to what is seen in America's backyard. This essay will outline how traditional agricultural practices have shifted to form a new agricultural landscape, which promotes the monoculture of crops through the overuse of chemicals and the mechanization of labor, as well as how the fair trade movement has provided an opposing and alternative method to contemporary farming.

To begin, the new agricultural landscape will be outlined, specifically discussing the significance of monoculture crops and how chemicals and machines assist in their production. The traditional Iowa farm in the United States was the home to "whole families of different plants and animal species, corn [which is a cash crop] only the fourth

most common . . . This diversity allowed the farm . . . to substantially

feed itself—and by that [Pollan does not] mean feed only the farmers,

but also the soil and the livestock" (Pollan 38). In traditional farming,

chemicals, fertilizers, and the use of technologically advanced

machinery were not required to feed families and communities.

However, a number of traditional farming practices had to be changed

in order to produce a monoculture of crops. For example, traditional

farmers rotated their crops and fallowed fields to allow the soil to be

replenished; if the soil was not replenished, its quality would decrease.

In contemporary agricultural farming, however, fertilizers are used that

add nutrients to the soil and improve its quality, thus keeping the land

in production for the same cash crop (Knight 188). With fertilizers being

added to the soil to replace natural nutrients, the crops produced are

not of the same quality as they once were—though the difference in

quality and potential health risks associated with monoculture are not

the sector's highest priorities. Therefore, traditional agriculture has

shifted from a self-sustaining business with a variety of crops toward

becoming a sector that both encourages and relies on a monoculture of

cash crops.

The "monoculture of farms, the increased size of farms, and the decline in variety of crops" are largely attributed to an emphasis on productivity that was not present before World War II (Knight 186). This increase in productivity can only be achieved by attempting to control the predictability of agriculture, which is extremely difficult given the unpredictability of soil and weather conditions. One way in which farmers increase predictability and thus increase a monoculture of crops is genetically engineering seeds to make crops appear very similar to one another. Another way to control the predictability of agriculture output, thus creating a monoculture of crops, is through the use of chemicals and machines. Knight contends that "industrial farming urges monoculture crops to be planted, irrigated, sprayed with chemicals, and machines to be used to harvest the crops. One cotton, soybean, or rice field appears to be identical to another" (187). Monoculture crops, therefore, could not be produced in the same quantities and with the same quality if chemicals and machines were not used at every level of crop production.

Chemicals and fertilizers, which are, indeed, used at almost every level in the production of cash crops in the United States, replace the traditional methods of farming—as discussed earlier—to create increased quantities of the monoculture cash crops. According to

Michael Pollan in *The Omnivore's Dilemma*

> the great turning point in the modern history of corn, which in
> turn marks a key turning point in the industrialization of . . .
> food, can be dated, with some precision, to the day, in 1947,
> when the huge munitions plant at Muscle Shoals, Alabama,
> switched over to making chemical fertilizer. (41)

Since chemical fertilizers were introduced in 1947, they have changed

the way of farming. In 1968, American farmers spread "nearly forty

million tons of chemical fertilizers or 260 pounds for each acre under

cultivation" (Berry 62). Without chemical fertilizers, a monoculture of

crops could not exist, because fertilizers add nutrients to the soil to

make crops grow faster and replenish the soil so that the same crops

can be planted in the same plots of land year after year (Knight 184).

Consequently, chemicals and fertilizer, despite being a potential risk to

the health of those who consume crops that have been sprayed with

chemicals or grown in fertilizer, are used in almost every aspect of

agricultural production in the United States and—more recently—in

developing nations. The use of chemicals and fertilizers is essential for

ensuring that a monoculture of crops is being produced more efficiently

and in larger quantities.

In addition to the overuse of chemicals, the mechanization of farming is also a contributor to the monoculture of crops that is currently seen across the agricultural landscape in the United States—a trend that is carrying over to developing nations. In contemporary agriculture, people are no longer responsible for the majority of the work; instead, machines have taken over. In *The Unsettling of America: Culture and Agriculture*, Wendell Berry argues that "the reduction of available manpower by each new machine created the need for a better machine or a different one" (59). Therefore, it would be extremely difficult to go back to a time when manpower was the primary source of labor in the agricultural business, which warrants the need for new and innovative machines that will help produce larger quantities of cash crops at a faster pace. In addition to the reduction of manpower in the sector, the farming and meat processing jobs that are left in the agricultural sector are "two of the most dangerous and low-paying jobs in the United States" (Knight 190). According to the Alabama Cooperative Extension System, "more than 700 deaths occurred in farming-related activities in 2003, and another 150,000 agricultural workers suffered disabling work-related injuries . . . Approximately 68% of the farm-related deaths can be traced to machinery" (Knight 190).

Though it is extremely problematic that what is left for farmers are the lowest-paying and most dangerous jobs in the United States, it is perhaps more problematic that this situation is not recognized by the majority of North Americans. The reduction of jobs in the agricultural sector because of machinery, as well as the state of those jobs, seems to go unnoticed, and, more importantly, these issues are not connected to the contemporary agricultural situation. Because the majority of deaths are machine-related, it becomes clear that worker deaths have not always been as high in the agricultural sector as they are now, having increased, in fact, because of the demand for additional and more technologically advanced machinery. Wendell Berry argues that there is no "acknowledgement of the 'monster,' technology, ('acre-eaters') on the soil, the produce, the farm communities, and the lives and characters of farmers" (61). Consequently, the mechanization of labor not only replaces human jobs but also disassociates humanity from the food production process.

It is important to understand how the agricultural sector has changed over time and why it encourages and promotes the monoculture of crops through the overuse of chemicals and the mechanization of labor, but it is also important to think about what agricultural practices might look like in the future and what the implications of those possible practices might be. One possibility for the future of the agriculture sector is that the control that agribusinesses have over large farms—but, more specifically, family farms—will continue to increase, making it almost impossible to grow crops outside of the monoculture cash crops that the sector wants to be grown. In *The Future of Food*, Deborah Koons discusses how Monsanto owns the patent for bioengineered seeds and how it sued Canadian farmers for patent infringement because they had crops with those seeds (usually due to cross-breeding or to the patented seeds being blown into fields not owned by Monsanto). Additionally, Monsanto requires farmers to sign license agreements to use their seeds, preventing them from re-using seeds in subsequent seasons. Perhaps the most troubling aspect of seed patenting for the future of agriculture is the creation of a new terminator seed. According to Andrew Knight, the terminator seed is "genetically engineered to prevent germination after a specific period of time and eliminates any option of seed saving" (189). If the terminator seed or its equivalent is released in the market, the family farm will have an extremely difficult time being able to grow cash crops, let alone any other crops. Another major possibility in the years to come is the "farms-of-the-future" or "model farms" concept, which many

people have started to build in the past several years. Wendell Berry

argues that

> The issue that is raised most directly by these "farms-of-the-future" is that of control. The ambition underlying these model farms is that of total control—a totally controlled agricultural environment . . . Therefore, if one is going to make a "model farm," one must give it a boundary, if possible a roof, that will keep out whatever does not "work." Weeds, insects, diseases do not work; leave them out. The weather works only sometimes, or on the average; leave the weather out. The work can be done by machines; leave the people out. But chemicals and drugs, no matter how dangerous, *do* work; they are part of the boundary, so they can be let in. (70-72)

This possibility for the future of agriculture essentially follows the

current model but creates what would happen if we continue down the

current path that the agriculture sector is on. Finally, and most

optimistically, there is a model for change within the contemporary

sector. The large industrial monoculture farms are not more efficient or

productive than family farms and are, in fact, extremely destructive to

rural economies (Knight 191). Family farms, however, are shown to be

more beneficial for communities, use more innovative marketing

strategies, and utilize natural resources better than larger monoculture

farms (191). With this model in mind, what can North Americans—and citizens of developing countries—do in order to ensure that model three is the model of the future? Fair trade is a viable solution to the contemporary agricultural situation and is currently combating monoculture crops, the overuse of chemicals in farming, and the mechanization of labor (including worker safety).

The fair trade movement is not intended to dismiss traditional—or even contemporary—practices across the agricultural landscape, but rather to critically analyze them and provide an alternative. The fair trade movement aims to provide "tangible benefits to small-scale farmers and workers, consumers, and the environment" (TransFair). These benefits are the primary focus of this paper because many of the benefits arise from trying to eliminate a monoculture of cash crops that exists largely due to an overuse of chemicals and the mechanization of labor. For example, the benefits for farmers and workers are largely associated with providing them with a fair price for their crops, a healthy and safe working environment, and a steady income. The problem is not whether the farmers are producing a cash crop; instead, the problem is that, within a monoculture of only cash crops, many farmers cannot earn a sustainable living because of the overflow of cash crops being produced, and the farmers who do not grow the monoculture cash crops are left out entirely. In *Fair Trade*, Brown argues that "production systems research should be carried out in collaboration with the producers to develop ways of combining cash crops and subsistence crops" (159). The demise of cash crops will not improve the agricultural system, but eliminating the monoculture of crops will increase the need to pay farmers from North America, as well as in developing nations, a fair price for the crops that they grow—whether they are cash crops or not.

The overuse of chemicals is also a concern for the fair trade movement, and the majority of fair trade products are certified organic. This certification means that the crops are not grown using chemicals or fertilizers, and that the quality and health of these crops are improved. According to Michael Barratt Brown

> The approach to alternative trading starts from bringing the producer to the consumer. This means asking what resources went into producing the goods, how they will affect the consumer's health and the health and very survival of the producers, what effect their production has on the environment and the balance of life on the planet. [This movement] is concerned that produce is grown organically and that animals are not ill-treated in the course of manufacturing products or producing food. But the main ideal behind this system of alternative trading is a concern for people—the subsistence

farmers who are the small-scale primary producers. (158)
By not using expensive chemicals and fertilizers and by growing organic crops, many of the farmers in North America and developing nations can once again afford to farm, and may even turn a profit from farming a diversity of crops.

Furthermore, many small-scale farmers cannot afford the expensive and innovative technology that large-scale farms can afford. This situation is especially true for small-scale farming in developing nations—the mechanization of labor replaces humans, provides unsafe working conditions for humans, administers large and unnecessary amounts of chemicals and fertilizers, supports a monoculture of crops, and disassociates humanity from the food production process. Despite all of this, however, the fair trade movement does not necessarily oppose the use of machinery, but its advocates hold the view that not being able to afford expensive and deadly machinery should not mean that small-scale farmers are not able to sell their crops. Fair trade-certified products "help build economic independence and empowerment for certified farmer cooperatives and their members," which is not possible with the increasing mechanization of labor in North America (158).

The fair trade movement is combating the mainstream contemporary agricultural system by providing an alternative. It aims to help small-scale farmers, who produce a diversity of crops, make a sustainable living while still participating in the trading system. The fair trade movement is, however, at a turning point. According to Nicholls and Opal's *Fair Trade: Market-Driven Ethical Consumption,*

> Fair trade is now entering the mainstream, trying to balance being "in and against" the market. The engagement of multinationals like Procter and Gamble and Starbucks . . . signs the commercial opportunity represented by fair trade. However, future development remains highly contested. (229)

If the fair trade movement is commercialized, it may very well lose its grassroots connections and no longer support small-scale farmers; however, if it does not, the movement may slowly dwindle away or not have the reach to make international and sustainable change in the agricultural landscape.

The agricultural landscape has undergone a tremendous shift since World War II. This shift gains more and more momentum each year, with a growing emphasis on monoculture cash crops, an increase in chemical and fertilizer use, and the mechanization of labor. This industrial system, which aims to increase efficiency and produce large quantities of cash crops, will only worsen over time, with more money and time being spent on bio-technology. The fair trade movement has risen to battle the contemporary agricultural landscape and provide consumers and farmers, in both North America and developing nations, the option of growing a diversity of crops and selling them at fair prices. This movement has achieved incredible growth in the past decade and is now at a crossroads, faced with upholding its grassroots campaigns or commercializing its operations. It is not known what is going to happen to the agricultural landscape; however, by purchasing fair trade-certified products, consumers can ensure that their voices are heard and that they can make a difference in contemporary farming.

APPENDIX TWO: EXAMPLE ESSAY WORKS CITED PAGE

Example essay work cited

Works Cited

Berry, Wendell. *The Unsettling of America: Culture and Agriculture*. San

Francisco: Sierra Club Books, 1996. Print.

Brown, Michael Barratt. *Fair Trade: Reform and Realities in the*

International Trading System. London: ZED Books, 1993. Print.

DeCarlo, Jacqueline. *Fair Trade: A Beginner's Guide*. Oxford: Oneworld

Publications, 2007. Print.

Knight, Andrew. "Supersizing Farms: The McDonaldization of

Agriculture." *McDonaldization: The Reader*. Ed. George Ritzer.

Thousand Oaks, London: Pine Forge Press, 2002. 183-96. Print.

Koons, Deborah. *The Future of Food*. Dir. Deborah Koons. Mill Valley:

Lily Films, 2004. DVD-ROM.

National Family Farm Coalition. *National Family Farm Coalition*. Web. 7

Apr. 2008. <http://www.nffc.net/issues/index.html>.

Nicholls, Alex, and Charlotte Opal. *Fair Trade: Market-Driven Ethical*

Consumption. Thousand Oaks, London, New Delhi: SAGE

Publications Ltd., 2005. Print.

Pollan, Michael. *The Omnivore's Dilemma: A Natural History of Four*

Meals. New York: Penguin, 2006. Print.

TransFair. *Fair Trade Certified…Guaranteed*. Web. 10 Mar. 2008.

<www.transfair.ca>.

Connect with Scribendi.com online:

Contact Scribendi.com: http://www.scribendi.com/contact

Twitter: http://twitter.com/Scribendi_Inc

Facebook: http://www.facebook.com/ScribendiInc

Scribendi.com's blog: http://www.scribendi.com/advice

ABOUT THE AUTHOR

Scribendi.com was founded in 1997 as one of the world's first online editing and proofreading companies. Based in Ontario, Canada, the company's primary goal is to provide clients with fast, reliable, and affordable revision services. Today, Scribendi.com is the world's largest online proofreading and editing company.

CPSIA information can be obtained
at www.ICGtesting.com
Printed in the USA
LVOW01s1748070416
482606LV00019B/804/P